revelation

revelation

authorised king james version

printed by authority

published by canongate

with an introduction by │ will self

First published in Great Britain in 1998
by Canongate Books Ltd
14 High Street, Edinburgh EH1 1TE

10 9 8 7 6 5 4 3 2

Introduction copyright © Will Self 1998
The moral right of the author has been asserted

British Library Cataloguing-in-Publication Data
A catalogue record is available on request from
the British Library

ISBN 0 86241 800 3

Typeset by Palimpsest Book Production
Book design by Paddy Cramsie
Printed and bound in Great Britain
by Caledonian International, Bishopbriggs

a note about pocket canons

The Authorised King James Version of the Bible, translated between 1603–11, coincided with an extraordinary flowering of English literature. This version, more than any other, and possibly more than any other work in history, has had an influence in shaping the language we speak and write today. Presenting individual books from the Bible as separate volumes, as they were originally conceived, encourages the reader to approach them as literary works in their own right.

The first twelve books in this series encompass categories as diverse as history, fiction, philosophy, love poetry and law. Each Pocket Canon also has its own introduction, specially commissioned from an impressive range of writers, which provides a personal interpretation of the text and explores its contemporary relevance.

Will Self is the author of The Quantity Theory of Insanity, *short-listed for the 1992 John Llewellyn Rhys Memorial Prize, winner of the 1993 Geoffrey Faber Memorial Prize. His books include* Cock & Bull, My Idea of Fun, Grey Area, Junk Mail, The Sweet Smell of Psychosis, Great Apes *and most recently* Tough, Tough Toys for Tough, Tough Boys.

introduction by will self

My friend Ben Trainin died thirteen years ago of a heart attack, brought on by an asthma attack, brought on by the complications of a compressed, involuted life: a decoction of existence. He and his girlfriend were living in a shoe box-shaped flat just off the Commercial Road in Whitechapel. The bed – where he died – was crammed under a window, from which you could see the plastic-wrapped schmutter in the windows across the road. Ben was twenty-eight.

He was not a simple soul – he was complex. He came from a convoluted family with connections both bohemian and East End. He'd gone up to Nottingham University to read history, but after doing too much amphetamine he was found giving an extempore, *al fresco* sermon, from the pulpit of the roof of his digs. He served drinks at the Colony Room club in Soho for the next couple of years, courtesy of his – self-styled – 'godfather' Ian Board. Then he took the Oxford general entrance paper and scored an unprecedented result. Interviewed by Christopher Hill – then still Master of Balliol – Ben was offered a place to read history. That's how we met.

Ben was fucking complex. Part of his act was to feign simplicity. Gap-toothed, tousle-haired, slack-jawed, he would gawp at me and intone 'Amazing!', 'No!', 'Really?' and 'Will!', before gurgling with giggles like an idiot. He walked with knees half bent, as if he were continually going downhill.

Ben was a giver of unexpected presents. I would be sitting in my room reading and Ben would silently tip-toe down on in. He'd deposit a book of Basho's poems, or a manual of Ch'an Zen teaching, then – still without speaking – he'd depart. From Ben I first heard the expression 'random acts of senseless generosity'.

He was brilliant and confused. One time he found me having a bad acid trip, prostrate on my bed, ensnared by a vision of an illimitable cathedral comprised entirely of screaming mouths. 'Bad trip,' he stated on seeing the state I was in. 'You need wine.' He poured two bottles of Burgundy down me, employing a furled magazine as a funnel. An hour later I was dancing to Edwin Starr's *Eye to Eye Contact*, at the Law Society disco.

Ben's maxim as far as drugs were concerned was 'little but often'. He constantly smoked tiny nuggets of hashish and snorted less than nugatory lines of amphetamine. With some like-minded souls we formed a rhythm and blues band. Ben loved Robert Johnson and might well have brokered a deal on his own soul in return for guitar-picking skill. Together we composed unlikely ditties. I loved him very much.

In the imbroglio of acid, speed, heroin, hashish, cocaine, philosophy, youth, literature, political protest, sex, friendship and dancing, Ben's mind frayed. The dissolution of our peer group seemed congruent with his own mind. When we left the university, Ben began to take day-returns from his own sanity. Then awaydays became bargain weekends. We pitched up in Brixton, squatting, in 1982. A very raw, very ragged time – especially for one who was frayed. One night Ben brandished a u-bend bicycle lock in my face and dared me to kill us both, batter us both to death. For someone who practised random acts of senseless generosity, the world had become a screaming, tight fist.

I saw Ben sporadically after that. He moved back to Kennington, a village a few miles outside Oxford. Initially he lived with a bizarre, obese character who was the local 'wise woman'. This was for real – I remember visiting him there and witnessing a sheepish young couple, who had come to consult her on the matter of fecundity. She was so fat she had a reinforced commode with an armchair of a seat. Ben said it was provided by the social services.

Then he moved in with a gay couple who were priests. They seemed caring men when I visited, and genuinely concerned for Ben's health and welfare, but there were nagging undertones – and even overtones – suggesting a less disinterested involvement on their part.

I was living in a borrowed flat in the Gloucester Road area during the hot, early summer of 1985. I had no money and expensive habits. One day Ben called and said he was coming over to see me for the first time in many months. In truth, I had begun to avoid him. The joint suicide attempt had been bad enough, but since then Ben had increasingly taken to interpreting the world through the dark glass of *The Book of Revelation*.

He carried a pocket bible – leather-bound as I recall – with him wherever he went. In the midst of always turbulent, disconnected discourses, he would wrench the tome out and brandishing it cite the applicable prophecy and provide his own piece of exegesis, which constituted impossibly spidery marginalia. Disturbingly his references were always correct – the last piece of mental viability left to him. Montaigne said: 'In my part of the country we call a man who has no memory "stupid".' Ben was never stupid. He spoke of the sharp two-edged sword (1:16), and the utility of communion with he who has 'the keys of hell and of death' (1:18).

Like many people who are teetering on the edge of psychosis – one foot rammed hard in the door of perception lest it slam shut forever – Ben found in *Revelation* an awful, immanent level of identification; an apparently fixed point around which his own frail psyche could orbit and then fission. Ben didn't subscribe to any, one view of the meaning of *Revelation* – he subscribed to them all.

I'm not certain that Ben's illness was ever adequately diagnosed. I do know that he was receiving some kind of help or treatment at the time of his death, but I don't think they'd yet managed to hammer this beautifully rounded persona into a square hole of psychopathology. My hunch is that he was manic-depressive. Perhaps now, with improved drugs, better cognitive approaches, Ben might have been saved – but I doubt it.

For there was an anguished level of insight in this man's disintegration. Even as he ran over – for the nth time – the precise equations that decoded the numerological content of *Revelation* – four beasts times seven seals, times twelve tribes of twelve thousand – he would still find himself hectored by the furies of his own reason, and pulling himself up short expostulate 'Of course, it's all a load of superstitious bollocks really.'

So Ben paced around the spacious, unpaid-for flat on this hot, early summer day. He wanted us to do *this* together, and to go *there*. He thought we ought to consider becoming *such-and-such*, or dedicating ourselves to this *particular* cause. And all of it was derived from *Revelation*, all of it was coextensive with – and tantamount to – the determined, ordained, god-directed universe.

He wanted me to go to the Natural History Museum with him, but I wouldn't. He scared me. When someone you love is veering in and out of sanity it's straightforwardly terrifying. They may have their foot rammed in the door, but if they let go the draught could suck you out of rationality along with them; expel you into a screaming void of the id.

Ben said goodbye to me, or rather he said he had come to say goodbye to me. He pocketed the small book of no calm and he left. He died a week later.

He wouldn't have – didn't – want to be in the condition he was. I believe he willed himself to death. On the despairing grapevine that sprang sad roots in the long hours immediately after his death, time and again I heard from other friends and lovers that Ben had been by that preceding week; that he had cropped up for the first time in months; that he had said he was coming to say goodbye – not simply said 'goodbye'.

A few months later I was ordering a takeaway in a fried chicken joint on Haverstock Hill when elements of a familiar litany came floating to me: an anti-prayerful, desperate incantation. It was the hulking man standing next to me in the queue, frayed jeans sagging open at the fly to reveal NHS issue

will self   xi pyjama bottoms underneath. We were – I internally acknowledged – within the crazily paved precincts of the Royal Free Hospital, that ziggurat of social hygiene. The man – who, nonpejoratively was clearly suffering from an array of schizoid symptoms – was speaking of that woman: 'And upon her forehead was a name written, MYSTERY, BABYLON THE GREAT, THE MOTHER OF HARLOTS AND ABOMINATIONS OF THE EARTH.'

His speech was Roman, then italicised, then capitalised. It was his own, private revelation.

I became, if not exactly fixated, at any rate intrigued by this seam of perverse Biblical exegesis, which was being squeezed out from the minds of the insane like variegated toothpaste ejected from a tube. I would lend an ear to any inapposite mutterer or street ranter I chanced upon, confident that in at least one out of three hits, there would be revelatory pay dirt.

I read *The Book of Revelation* once – I never wanted to read it again. I found it a sick text. Perhaps it's the occlusion of judgmental types, and the congruent occlusion of psyches, but there's something *not quite right* about *Revelation*. I feel it as an insemination of older, more primal verities into an as yet fresh dough of syncretism – the NeoPlatonists still kneading at the stuff of the messiah. The riot of violent, imagistic occurrences; the cabalistic emphasis on numbers; the visceral repulsion expressed towards the bodily, the sensual and the sexual. It deranges in and of itself, and sets the parameters, marshals the props, for all the excessive playlets to come. In its vile obscurantism is its baneful effect; the original language may have welded the metaphoric with the signified, the *logos* with the flesh, but in the King James version the text is a guignol of tedium, a portentous horror film.

I have read the exegetical texts on *Revelation* and I have read the book itself several more times. I feel no closer to understanding what it is about. Not in the obvious senses – I appreciate the status of Hebraic and early Christian prophecy as pure revelation, decoupled from the mere temporal causality, spatial contiguity – but in the sense that I cannot empathise with this piece of writing, I cannot feel what it might be like to feel it.

Last night I plugged into the internet and went looking for *Revelation*. Funny how the dead get deader. Ben was dead from the moment he died, but five years after his death he was deader, and now he's deader still. I know this because of the anachronistic quality of my vision of him: if he were to be resurrected now, he would look out of place next to my full colour VDU screen, with its weary emphasis that what you see is what you get.

I keyed it into a not especially vigorous search engine, keyed in the bald awfulness of it: *The Book of Revelation*. Hit the return key and waited. The screen departed as a scroll when it is rolled together and I was offered a choice of 2,666,896 web sites. And these were by no means all 'Top 10 Revelations in Marcia Clark's New Book'. Oh no, if only. No, they were the real McCoy: the apocalyptic visions visited on the wired generation in the here and now of Christian-defined 1998. They no longer have to mutter in fast food outlets, they no longer have to address themselves to bare precincts, their only witnesses scurrying fast in the opposite direction. Now they can make the screen depart as a scroll when it is rolled together.

Our sense of the apocalypse is steeped in the language of *Revelation*. In this century the star called Wormwood *has* fallen, and the sea has become as black as sackcloth of hair, and the moon has become as blood. We have heard the silence – about the space of half an hour – that accompanied the opening of the seventh seal, yet still we are here.

I have no truck with personal immortality – it is the dross of the opium of the people. I have no time for the conception of humans as born in sin, screaming for redemption. If *Revelation* conjures up one single feeling in me, as we stand on the cusp of a new millennium, awaiting television retrospectives that will occupy the space of many hours, it is one of superstitious awe, 'Look on my works, ye Mighty, and despair'. To think this ancient text has survived to be the very stuff of modern, psychotic nightmare.

Not only the good die young – but some do.

In memory of Benjamin Gregor Trainin, 1957–85

the revelation of st john the divine

The Revelation of Jesus Christ, which God gave unto him, to
shew unto his servants things which must shortly come to
pass; and he sent and signified it by his angel unto his servant John, ²who bare record of the word of God, and of the
testimony of Jesus Christ, and of all things that he saw.
³Blessed is he that readeth, and they that hear the words of
this prophecy, and keep those things which are written
therein; for the time is at hand.

⁴John to the seven churches which are in Asia: Grace be
unto you, and peace, from him which is, and which was, and
which is to come; and from the seven Spirits which are before
his throne; ⁵and from Jesus Christ, who is the faithful witness,
and the first begotten of the dead, and the prince of the kings
of the earth. Unto him that loved us, and washed us from our
sins in his own blood, ⁶and hath made us kings and priests
unto God and his Father; to him be glory and dominion for ever
and ever. Amen. ⁷Behold, he cometh with clouds; and every
eye shall see him, and they also which pierced him; and all
kindreds of the earth shall wail because of him. Even so, Amen.

⁸'I am Alpha and Omega, the beginning and the ending,'
saith the Lord, which is, and which was, and which is to come,
the Almighty. ⁹I John, who also am your brother, and com-
panion in tribulation, and in the kingdom and patience of

Jesus Christ, was in the isle that is called Patmos, for the word of God, and for the testimony of Jesus Christ. [10] I was in the Spirit on the Lord's day, and heard behind me a great voice, as of a trumpet, [11] saying, 'I am Alpha and Omega, the first and the last'; and, 'What thou seest, write in a book, and send it unto the seven churches which are in Asia; unto Ephesus, and unto Smyrna, and unto Pergamos, and unto Thyatira, and unto Sardis, and unto Philadelphia, and unto Laodicea.'

[12] And I turned to see the voice that spake with me. And being turned, I saw seven golden candlesticks; [13] and in the midst of the seven candlesticks one like unto the Son of man, clothed with a garment down to the foot, and girt about the paps with a golden girdle. [14] His head and his hairs were white like wool, as white as snow; and his eyes were as a flame of fire; [15] and his feet like unto fine brass, as if they burned in a furnace; and his voice as the sound of many waters. [16] And he had in his right hand seven stars; and out of his mouth went a sharp twoedged sword; and his countenance was as the sun shineth in his strength.

[17] And when I saw him, I fell at his feet as dead. And he laid his right hand upon me, saying unto me, 'Fear not; I am the first and the last: [18] I am he that liveth, and was dead; and, behold, I am alive for evermore, Amen; and have the keys of hell and of death. [19] Write the things which thou hast seen, and the things which are, and the things which shall be hereafter; [20] the mystery of the seven stars which thou sawest in my right hand, and the seven golden candlesticks. The seven stars are the angels of the seven churches; and the seven candlesticks which thou sawest are the seven churches.'

2 'Unto the angel of the church of Ephesus write: These things saith he that holdeth the seven stars in his right hand, who walketh in the midst of the seven golden candlesticks: ²I know thy works, and thy labour, and thy patience, and how thou canst not bear them which are evil; and thou hast tried them which say they are apostles, and are not, and hast found them liars; ³and hast borne, and hast patience, and for my name's sake hast laboured, and hast not fainted. ⁴Nevertheless I have somewhat against thee, because thou hast left thy first love. ⁵Remember therefore from whence thou art fallen, and repent, and do the first works; or else I will come unto thee quickly, and will remove thy candlestick out of his place, except thou repent. ⁶But this thou hast, that thou hatest the deeds of the Nicolaitans, which I also hate. ⁷He that hath an ear, let him hear what the Spirit saith unto the churches; to him that overcometh will I give to eat of the tree of life, which is in the midst of the paradise of God.

⁸'And unto the angel of the church in Smyrna write: These things saith the first and the last, which was dead, and is alive: ⁹I know thy works, and tribulation, and poverty (but thou art rich), and I know the blasphemy of them which say they are Jews, and are not, but are the synagogue of Satan. ¹⁰Fear none of those things which thou shalt suffer. Behold, the devil shall cast some of you into prison, that ye may be tried; and ye shall have tribulation ten days; be thou faithful unto death, and I will give thee a crown of life. ¹¹He that hath an ear, let him hear what the Spirit saith unto the churches; he that overcometh shall not be hurt of the second death.

¹²'And to the angel of the church in Pergamos write: These

things saith he which hath the sharp sword with two edges: ¹³ I know thy works, and where thou dwellest, even where Satan's seat is; and thou holdest fast my name, and hast not denied my faith, even in those days wherein Antipas was my faithful martyr, who was slain among you, where Satan dwelleth. ¹⁴ But I have a few things against thee, because thou hast there them that hold the doctrine of Balaam, who taught Balac to cast a stumblingblock before the children of Israel, to eat things sacrificed unto idols, and to commit fornication. ¹⁵ So hast thou also them that hold the doctrine of the Nicolaitans, which thing I hate. ¹⁶ Repent; or else I will come unto thee quickly, and will fight against them with the sword of my mouth. ¹⁷ He that hath an ear, let him hear what the Spirit saith unto the churches; to him that overcometh will I give to eat of the hidden manna, and will give him a white stone, and in the stone a new name written, which no man knoweth saving he that receiveth it.

¹⁸ 'And unto the angel of the church in Thyatira write: These things saith the Son of God, who hath his eyes like unto a flame of fire, and his feet are like fine brass: ¹⁹ I know thy works, and charity, and service, and faith, and thy patience, and thy works; and the last to be more than the first. ²⁰ Notwithstanding I have a few things against thee, because thou sufferest that woman Jezebel, which calleth herself a prophetess, to teach and to seduce my servants to commit fornication, and to eat things sacrificed unto idols. ²¹ And I gave her space to repent of her fornication; and she repented not. ²² Behold, I will cast her into a bed, and them that commit adultery with her into great tribulation, except they repent

of their deeds. ²³And I will kill her children with death; and all the churches shall know that I am he which searcheth the reins and hearts; and I will give unto every one of you according to your works. ²⁴But unto you I say, and unto the rest in Thyatira, as many as have not this doctrine, and which have not known the depths of Satan, as they speak; I will put upon you none other burden. ²⁵But that which ye have already hold fast till I come. ²⁶And he that overcometh, and keepeth my works unto the end, to him will I give power over the nations; ²⁷and he shall rule them with a rod of iron; as the vessels of a potter shall they be broken to shivers; even as I received of my Father. ²⁸And I will give him the morning star. ²⁹He that hath an ear, let him hear what the Spirit saith unto the churches.

3 'And unto the angel of the church in Sardis write: These things saith he that hath the seven Spirits of God, and the seven stars: I know thy works, that thou hast a name that thou livest, and art dead. ²Be watchful, and strengthen the things which remain, that are ready to die; for I have not found thy works perfect before God. ³Remember therefore how thou hast received and heard, and hold fast, and repent. If therefore thou shalt not watch, I will come on thee as a thief, and thou shalt not know what hour I will come upon thee. ⁴Thou hast a few names even in Sardis which have not defiled their garments; and they shall walk with me in white; for they are worthy. ⁵He that overcometh, the same shall be clothed in white raiment; and I will not blot out his name out of the book of life, but I will confess his name before my Father, and before his angels. ⁶He that hath an ear, let him hear what the Spirit saith unto the churches.

⁷'And to the angel of the church in Philadelphia write: These things saith he that is holy, he that is true, he that hath the key of David, he that openeth, and no man shutteth; and shutteth, and no man openeth: ⁸I know thy works; behold, I have set before thee an open door, and no man can shut it; for thou hast a little strength, and hast kept my word, and hast not denied my name. ⁹Behold, I will make them of the synagogue of Satan, which say they are Jews, and are not, but do lie; behold, I will make them to come and worship before thy feet, and to know that I have loved thee. ¹⁰Because thou hast kept the word of my patience, I also will keep thee from the hour of temptation, which shall come upon all the world, to try them that dwell upon the earth. ¹¹Behold, I

come quickly; hold that fast which thou hast, that no man take thy crown. ¹² Him that overcometh will I make a pillar in the temple of my God, and he shall go no more out: and I will write upon him the name of my God, and the name of the city of my God, which is new Jerusalem, which cometh down out of heaven from my God; and I will write upon him my new name. ¹³ He that hath an ear, let him hear what the Spirit saith unto the churches.

¹⁴ 'And unto the angel of the church of the Laodiceans write: These things saith the Amen, the faithful and true witness, the beginning of the creation of God: ¹⁵ I know thy works, that thou art neither cold nor hot; I would thou wert cold or hot. ¹⁶ So then because thou art lukewarm, and neither cold nor hot, I will spue thee out of my mouth. ¹⁷ Because thou sayest, "I am rich, and increased with goods, and have need of nothing"; and knowest not that thou art wretched, and miserable, and poor, and blind, and naked. ¹⁸ I counsel thee to buy of me gold tried in the fire, that thou mayest be rich; and white raiment, that thou mayest be clothed, and that the shame of thy nakedness do not appear; and anoint thine eyes with eyesalve, that thou mayest see. ¹⁹ As many as I love, I rebuke and chasten: be zealous therefore, and repent. ²⁰ Behold, I stand at the door, and knock: if any man hear my voice, and open the door, I will come in to him, and will sup with him, and he with me. ²¹ To him that overcometh will I grant to sit with me in my throne, even as I also overcame, and am set down with my Father in his throne. ²² He that hath an ear, let him hear what the Spirit saith unto the churches.'

4 After this I looked, and, behold, a door was opened in heaven; and the first voice which I heard was as it were of a trumpet talking with me; which said, 'Come up hither, and I will shew thee things which must be hereafter.' ²And immediately I was in the spirit; and, behold, a throne was set in heaven, and one sat on the throne. ³And he that sat was to look upon like a jasper and a sardine stone; and there was a rainbow round about the throne, in sight like unto an emerald. ⁴And round about the throne were four and twenty seats; and upon the seats I saw four and twenty elders sitting, clothed in white raiment; and they had on their heads crowns of gold. ⁵And out of the throne proceeded lightnings and thunderings and voices; and there were seven lamps of fire burning before the throne, which are the seven Spirits of God. ⁶And before the throne there was a sea of glass like unto crystal; and in the midst of the throne, and round about the throne, were four beasts full of eyes before and behind. ⁷And the first beast was like a lion, and the second beast like a calf, and the third beast had a face as a man, and the fourth beast was like a flying eagle. ⁸And the four beasts had each of them six wings about him; and they were full of eyes within; and they rest not day and night, saying, 'Holy, holy, holy, Lord God Almighty, which was, and is, and is to come.' ⁹And when those beasts give glory and honour and thanks to him that sat on the throne, who liveth for ever and ever, ¹⁰ the four and twenty elders fall down before him that sat on the throne, and worship him that liveth for ever and ever, and cast their crowns before the throne, saying, ¹¹'Thou art worthy, O Lord, to receive glory and honour and power; for thou hast created all things, and for thy pleasure they are and were created.'

5 And I saw in the right hand of him that sat on the throne a book written within and on the backside, sealed with seven seals. ²And I saw a strong angel proclaiming with a loud voice, 'Who is worthy to open the book, and to loose the seals thereof?' ³And no man in heaven, nor in earth, neither under the earth, was able to open the book, neither to look thereon. ⁴And I wept much, because no man was found worthy to open and to read the book, neither to look thereon. ⁵And one of the elders saith unto me, 'Weep not; behold, the Lion of the tribe of Juda, the Root of David, hath prevailed to open the book, and to loose the seven seals thereof.'

⁶And I beheld, and, lo, in the midst of the throne and of the four beasts, and in the midst of the elders, stood a Lamb as it had been slain, having seven horns and seven eyes, which are the seven Spirits of God sent forth into all the earth. ⁷And he came and took the book out of the right hand of him that sat upon the throne. ⁸And when he had taken the book, the four beasts and four and twenty elders fell down before the Lamb, having every one of them harps, and golden vials full of odours, which are the prayers of saints. ⁹And they sung a new song, saying,

> Thou art worthy to take the book,
>> and to open the seals thereof;
>>> for thou wast slain, and hast redeemed us
>> to God by thy blood out of every kindred,
>>> and tongue, and people, and nation;
> ¹⁰and hast made us unto our God kings and priests;
>> and we shall reign on the earth.

¹¹And I beheld, and I heard the voice of many angels round about the throne and the beasts and the elders: and the number of them was ten thousand times ten thousand, and thousands of thousands; ¹²saying with a loud voice, 'Worthy is the Lamb that was slain to receive power, and riches, and wisdom, and strength, and honour, and glory, and blessing.' ¹³And every creature which is in heaven, and on the earth, and under the earth, and such as are in the sea, and all that are in them, heard I saying, 'Blessing, and honour, and glory, and power, be unto him that sitteth upon the throne, and unto the Lamb for ever and ever.' ¹⁴And the four beasts said, 'Amen.' And the four and twenty elders fell down and worshipped him that liveth for ever and ever.

6 And I saw when the Lamb opened one of the seals, and I heard, as it were the noise of thunder, one of the four beasts saying, 'Come and see.' ²And I saw, and behold a white horse; and he that sat on him had a bow; and a crown was given unto him; and he went forth conquering, and to conquer.

³And when he had opened the second seal, I heard the second beast say, 'Come and see.' ⁴And there went out another horse that was red; and power was given to him that sat thereon to take peace from the earth, and that they should kill one another: and there was given unto him a great sword.

⁵And when he had opened the third seal, I heard the third beast say, 'Come and see.' And I beheld, and lo a black horse; and he that sat on him had a pair of balances in his hand. ⁶And I heard a voice in the midst of the four beasts say, 'A measure of wheat for a penny, and three measures of barley for a penny; and see thou hurt not the oil and the wine.'

⁷And when he had opened the fourth seal, I heard the voice of the fourth beast say, 'Come and see.' ⁸And I looked, and behold a pale horse; and his name that sat on him was Death, and Hell followed with him. And power was given unto them over the fourth part of the earth, to kill with sword, and with hunger, and with death, and with the beasts of the earth.

⁹And when he had opened the fifth seal, I saw under the altar the souls of them that were slain for the word of God, and for the testimony which they held. ¹⁰And they cried with a loud voice, saying, 'How long, O Lord, holy and true, dost thou not judge and avenge our blood on them that dwell on the earth?' ¹¹And white robes were given unto every one of

them; and it was said unto them that they should rest yet for a little season, until their fellowservants also and their brethren, that should be killed as they were, should be fulfilled.

¹²And I beheld when he had opened the sixth seal, and, lo, there was a great earthquake; and the sun became black as sackcloth of hair, and the moon became as blood; ¹³and the stars of heaven fell unto the earth, even as a fig tree casteth her untimely figs, when she is shaken of a mighty wind. ¹⁴And the heaven departed as a scroll when it is rolled together; and every mountain and island were moved out of their places. ¹⁵And the kings of the earth, and the great men, and the rich men, and the chief captains, and the mighty men, and every bondman, and every free man, hid themselves in the dens and in the rocks of the mountains; ¹⁶and said to the mountains and rocks, 'Fall on us, and hide us from the face of him that sitteth on the throne, and from the wrath of the Lamb; ¹⁷for the great day of his wrath is come, and who shall be able to stand?'

7 And after these things I saw four angels standing on the four corners of the earth, holding the four winds of the earth, that the wind should not blow on the earth, nor on the sea, nor on any tree. ²And I saw another angel ascending from the east, having the seal of the living God; and he cried with a loud voice to the four angels, to whom it was given to hurt the earth and the sea, ³saying, 'Hurt not the earth, neither the sea, nor the trees, till we have sealed the servants of our God in their foreheads.'

⁴And I heard the number of them which were sealed; and there were sealed an hundred and forty and four thousand of all the tribes of the children of Israel. ⁵Of the tribe of Juda were sealed twelve thousand. Of the tribe of Reuben were sealed twelve thousand. Of the tribe of Gad were sealed twelve thousand. ⁶Of the tribe of Aser were sealed twelve thousand. Of the tribe of Nepthalim were sealed twelve thousand. Of the tribe of Manasses were sealed twelve thousand. ⁷Of the tribe of Simeon were sealed twelve thousand. Of the tribe of Levi were sealed twelve thousand. Of the tribe of Issachar were sealed twelve thousand. ⁸Of the tribe of Zabulon were sealed twelve thousand. Of the tribe of Joseph were sealed twelve thousand. Of the tribe of Benjamin were sealed twelve thousand.

⁹After this I beheld, and, lo, a great multitude, which no man could number, of all nations, and kindreds, and people, and tongues, stood before the throne, and before the Lamb, clothed with white robes, and palms in their hands; ¹⁰and cried with a loud voice, saying, 'Salvation to our God which sitteth upon the throne, and unto the Lamb.'

¹¹And all the angels stood round about the throne, and about the elders and the four beasts, and fell before the throne on their faces, and worshipped God, ¹²saying, 'Amen: Blessing, and glory, and wisdom, and thanksgiving, and honour, and power, and might, be unto our God for ever and ever. Amen.'

¹³And one of the elders answered, saying unto me, 'What are these which are arrayed in white robes? And whence came they?' ¹⁴And I said unto him, 'Sir, thou knowest.' And he said to me, 'These are they which came out of great tribulation, and have washed their robes, and made them white in the blood of the Lamb. ¹⁵Therefore are they before the throne of God, and serve him day and night in his temple; and he that sitteth on the throne shall dwell among them. ¹⁶They shall hunger no more, neither thirst any more; neither shall the sun light on them, nor any heat. ¹⁷For the Lamb which is in the midst of the throne shall feed them, and shall lead them unto living fountains of waters; and God shall wipe away all tears from their eyes.'

8 And when he had opened the seventh seal, there was silence in heaven about the space of half an hour. ²And I saw the seven angels which stood before God; and to them were given seven trumpets.

³And another angel came and stood at the altar, having a golden censer; and there was given unto him much incense, that he should offer it with the prayers of all saints upon the golden altar which was before the throne. ⁴And the smoke of the incense, which came with the prayers of the saints, ascended up before God out of the angel's hand. ⁵And the angel took the censer, and filled it with fire of the altar, and cast it into the earth; and there were voices, and thunderings, and lightnings, and an earthquake.

⁶And the seven angels which had the seven trumpets prepared themselves to sound.

⁷ The first angel sounded, and there followed hail and fire mingled with blood, and they were cast upon the earth; and the third part of trees was burnt up, and all green grass was burnt up.

⁸And the second angel sounded, and as it were a great mountain burning with fire was cast into the sea; and the third part of the sea became blood; ⁹and the third part of the creatures which were in the sea, and had life, died; and the third part of the ships were destroyed.

¹⁰And the third angel sounded, and there fell a great star from heaven, burning as it were a lamp, and it fell upon the third part of the rivers, and upon the fountains of waters; ¹¹and the name of the star is called Wormwood; and the third part of the waters became wormwood; and many men died

of the waters, because they were made bitter.

[12]And the fourth angel sounded, and the third part of the sun was smitten, and the third part of the moon, and the third part of the stars; so as the third part of them was darkened, and the day shone not for a third part of it, and the night likewise.

[13]And I beheld, and heard an angel flying through the midst of heaven, saying with a loud voice, 'Woe, woe, woe, to the inhabiters of the earth by reason of the other voices of the trumpet of the three angels, which are yet to sound!'

9 And the fifth angel sounded, and I saw a star fall from heaven unto the earth; and to him was given the key of the bottomless pit. ²And he opened the bottomless pit; and there arose a smoke out of the pit, as the smoke of a great furnace; and the sun and the air were darkened by reason of the smoke of the pit. ³And there came out of the smoke locusts upon the earth; and unto them was given power, as the scorpions of the earth have power. ⁴And it was commanded them that they should not hurt the grass of the earth, neither any green thing, neither any tree; but only those men which have not the seal of God in their foreheads. ⁵And to them it was given that they should not kill them, but that they should be tormented five months; and their torment was as the torment of a scorpion, when he striketh a man. ⁶And in those days shall men seek death, and shall not find it; and shall desire to die, and death shall flee from them.

⁷And the shapes of the locusts were like unto horses prepared unto battle; and on their heads were as it were crowns like gold, and their faces were as the faces of men. ⁸And they had hair as the hair of women, and their teeth were as the teeth of lions. ⁹And they had breastplates, as it were breastplates of iron; and the sound of their wings was as the sound of chariots of many horses running to battle. ¹⁰And they had tails like unto scorpions, and there were stings in their tails; and their power was to hurt men five months. ¹¹And they had a king over them, which is the angel of the bottomless pit, whose name in the Hebrew tongue is Abaddon, but in the Greek tongue hath his name Apollyon.

¹²One woe is past; and, behold, there come two woes

more hereafter. ¹³And the sixth angel sounded, and I heard a voice from the four horns of the golden altar which is before God, ¹⁴saying to the sixth angel which had the trumpet, 'Loose the four angels which are bound in the great river Euphrates.' ¹⁵And the four angels were loosed, which were prepared for an hour, and a day, and a month, and a year, for to slay the third part of men. ¹⁶And the number of the army of the horsemen were two hundred thousand thousand: and I heard the number of them. ¹⁷And thus I saw the horses in the vision, and them that sat on them, having breast-plates of fire, and of jacinth, and brimstone; and the heads of the horses were as the heads of lions; and out of their mouths issued fire and smoke and brimstone. ¹⁸By these three was the third part of men killed, by the fire, and by the smoke, and by the brimstone, which issued out of their mouths. ¹⁹For their power is in their mouth, and in their tails; for their tails were like unto serpents, and had heads, and with them they do hurt.

²⁰And the rest of the men which were not killed by these plagues yet repented not of the works of their hands, that they should not worship devils, and idols of gold, and silver, and brass, and stone, and of wood; which neither can see, nor hear, nor walk; ²¹neither repented they of their murders, nor of their sorceries, nor of their fornication, nor of their thefts.

10

And I saw another mighty angel come down from heaven, clothed with a cloud; and a rainbow was upon his head, and his face was as it were the sun, and his feet as pillars of fire; ²and he had in his hand a little book open; and he set his right foot upon the sea, and his left foot on the earth, ³and cried with a loud voice, as when a lion roareth; and when he had cried, seven thunders uttered their voices. ⁴And when the seven thunders had uttered their voices, I was about to write; and I heard a voice from heaven saying unto me, 'Seal up those things which the seven thunders uttered, and write them not.' ⁵And the angel which I saw stand upon the sea and upon the earth lifted up his hand to heaven, ⁶and sware by him that liveth for ever and ever, who created heaven, and the things that therein are, and the earth, and the things that therein are, and the sea, and the things which are therein, that there should be time no longer; ⁷but in the days of the voice of the seventh angel, when he shall begin to sound, the mystery of God should be finished, as he hath declared to his servants the prophets.

⁸And the voice which I heard from heaven spake unto me again, and said, 'Go and take the little book which is open in the hand of the angel which standeth upon the sea and upon the earth.' ⁹And I went unto the angel, and said unto him, 'Give me the little book.' And he said unto me, 'Take it, and eat it up; and it shall make thy belly bitter, but it shall be in thy mouth sweet as honey.' ¹⁰And I took the little book out of the angel's hand, and ate it up; and it was in my mouth sweet as honey; and as soon as I had eaten it, my belly was bitter.

¹¹And he said unto me, 'Thou must prophesy again before many peoples, and nations, and tongues, and kings.'

11 And there was given me a reed like unto a rod; and the angel stood, saying, 'Rise, and measure the temple of God, and the altar, and them that worship therein. ²But the court which is without the temple leave out, and measure it not; for it is given unto the Gentiles; and the holy city shall they tread under foot forty and two months. ³And I will give power unto my two witnesses, and they shall prophesy a thousand two hundred and threescore days, clothed in sackcloth.'

⁴These are the two olive trees, and the two candlesticks standing before the God of the earth. ⁵And if any man will hurt them, fire proceedeth out of their mouth, and devoureth their enemies; and if any man will hurt them, he must in this manner be killed. ⁶These have power to shut heaven, that it rain not in the days of their prophecy; and have power over waters to turn them to blood, and to smite the earth with all plagues, as often as they will.

⁷And when they shall have finished their testimony, the beast that ascendeth out of the bottomless pit shall make war against them, and shall overcome them, and kill them. ⁸And their dead bodies shall lie in the street of the great city, which spiritually is called Sodom and Egypt, where also our Lord was crucified. ⁹And they of the people and kindreds and tongues and nations shall see their dead bodies three days and an half, and shall not suffer their dead bodies to be put in graves. ¹⁰And they that dwell upon the earth shall rejoice over them, and make merry, and shall send gifts one to another; because these two prophets tormented them that dwelt on the earth.

¹¹And after three days and an half the Spirit of life from

God entered into them, and they stood upon their feet; and great fear fell upon them which saw them. ¹²And they heard a great voice from heaven saying unto them, 'Come up hither.' And they ascended up to heaven in a cloud; and their enemies beheld them. ¹³And the same hour was there a great earthquake, and the tenth part of the city fell, and in the earthquake were slain of men seven thousand; and the remnant were affrighted, and gave glory to the God of heaven.

¹⁴The second woe is past; and, behold, the third woe cometh quickly.

¹⁵And the seventh angel sounded; and there were great voices in heaven, saying, 'The kingdoms of this world are become the kingdoms of our Lord, and of his Christ; and he shall reign for ever and ever.'

¹⁶And the four and twenty elders, which sat before God on their seats, fell upon their faces, and worshipped God, ¹⁷saying, 'We give thee thanks, O Lord God Almighty, which art, and wast, and art to come; because thou hast taken to thee thy great power, and hast reigned. ¹⁸And the nations were angry, and thy wrath is come, and the time of the dead, that they should be judged, and that thou shouldest give reward unto thy servants the prophets, and to the saints, and them that fear thy name, small and great; and shouldest destroy them which destroy the earth.'

¹⁹And the temple of God was opened in heaven, and there was seen in his temple the ark of his testament; and there were lightnings, and voices, and thunderings, and an earthquake, and great hail.

12 And there appeared a great wonder in heaven; a woman clothed with the sun, and the moon under her feet, and upon her head a crown of twelve stars; ²and she being with child cried, travailing in birth, and pained to be delivered. ³And there appeared another wonder in heaven; and behold a great red dragon, having seven heads and ten horns, and seven crowns upon his heads. ⁴And his tail drew the third part of the stars of heaven, and did cast them to the earth; and the dragon stood before the woman which was ready to be delivered, for to devour her child as soon as it was born. ⁵And she brought forth a man child, who was to rule all nations with a rod of iron; and her child was caught up unto God, and to his throne. ⁶And the woman fled into the wilderness, where she hath a place prepared of God, that they should feed her there a thousand two hundred and threescore days.

⁷And there was war in heaven: Michael and his angels fought against the dragon; and the dragon fought and his angels, ⁸and prevailed not; neither was their place found any more in heaven. ⁹And the great dragon was cast out, that old serpent, called the Devil, and Satan, which deceiveth the whole world: he was cast out into the earth, and his angels were cast out with him.

¹⁰And I heard a loud voice saying in heaven, 'Now is come salvation, and strength, and the kingdom of our God, and the power of his Christ; for the accuser of our brethren is cast down, which accused them before our God day and night. ¹¹And they overcame him by the blood of the Lamb, and by the word of their testimony; and they loved not their

lives unto the death. ¹²Therefore rejoice, ye heavens, and ye that dwell in them. Woe to the inhabiters of the earth and of the sea! For the devil is come down unto you, having great wrath, because he knoweth that he hath but a short time.'

¹³And when the dragon saw that he was cast unto the earth, he persecuted the woman which brought forth the man child. ¹⁴And to the woman were given two wings of a great eagle, that she might fly into the wilderness, into her place, where she is nourished for a time, and times, and half a time, from the face of the serpent. ¹⁵And the serpent cast out of his mouth water as a flood after the woman, that he might cause her to be carried away of the flood. ¹⁶And the earth helped the woman, and the earth opened her mouth, and swallowed up the flood which the dragon cast out of his mouth. ¹⁷And the dragon was wroth with the woman, and went to make war with the remnant of her seed, which keep the commandments of God, and have the testimony of Jesus Christ.

13 And I stood upon the sand of the sea, and saw a beast rise up out of the sea, having seven heads and ten horns, and upon his horns ten crowns, and upon his heads the name of blasphemy. ²And the beast which I saw was like unto a leopard, and his feet were as the feet of a bear, and his mouth as the mouth of a lion; and the dragon gave him his power, and his seat, and great authority. ³And I saw one of his heads as it were wounded to death; and his deadly wound was healed; and all the world wondered after the beast. ⁴And they worshipped the dragon which gave power unto the beast; and they worshipped the beast, saying, 'Who is like unto the beast? Who is able to make war with him?'

⁵And there was given unto him a mouth speaking great things and blasphemies; and power was given unto him to continue forty and two months. ⁶And he opened his mouth in blasphemy against God, to blaspheme his name, and his tabernacle, and them that dwell in heaven. ⁷And it was given unto him to make war with the saints, and to overcome them; and power was given him over all kindreds, and tongues, and nations. ⁸And all that dwell upon the earth shall worship him, whose names are not written in the book of life of the Lamb slain from the foundation of the world.

⁹If any man have an ear, let him hear. ¹⁰He that leadeth into captivity shall go into captivity; he that killeth with the sword must be killed with the sword. Here is the patience and the faith of the saints.

¹¹And I beheld another beast coming up out of the earth; and he had two horns like a lamb, and he spake as a dragon. ¹²And he exerciseth all the power of the first beast before

him, and causeth the earth and them which dwell therein to worship the first beast, whose deadly wound was healed. [13]And he doeth great wonders, so that he maketh fire come down from heaven on the earth in the sight of men, [14]and deceiveth them that dwell on the earth by the means of those miracles which he had power to do in the sight of the beast; saying to them that dwell on the earth that they should make an image to the beast, which had the wound by a sword, and did live. [15]And he had power to give life unto the image of the beast, that the image of the beast should both speak, and cause that as many as would not worship the image of the beast should be killed. [16]And he causeth all, both small and great, rich and poor, free and bond, to receive a mark in their right hand, or in their foreheads; [17]and that no man might buy or sell, save he that had the mark, or the name of the beast, or the number of his name. [18]Here is wisdom. Let him that hath understanding count the number of the beast; for it is the number of a man; and his number is six hundred threescore and six.

14 And I looked, and, lo, a Lamb stood on the mount Sion, and with him an hundred forty and four thousand, having his Father's name written in their foreheads. ²And I heard a voice from heaven, as the voice of many waters, and as the voice of a great thunder; and I heard the voice of harpers harping with their harps; ³ and they sung as it were a new song before the throne, and before the four beasts, and the elders; and no man could learn that song but the hundred and forty and four thousand, which were redeemed from the earth. ⁴These are they which were not defiled with women; for they are virgins. These are they which follow the Lamb whithersoever he goeth. These were redeemed from among men, being the firstfruits unto God and to the Lamb. ⁵And in their mouth was found no guile; for they are without fault before the throne of God.

⁶And I saw another angel fly in the midst of heaven, having the everlasting gospel to preach unto them that dwell on the earth, and to every nation, and kindred, and tongue, and people, ⁷saying with a loud voice, 'Fear God, and give glory to him, for the hour of his judgment is come; and worship him that made heaven, and earth, and the sea, and the fountains of waters.'

⁸And there followed another angel, saying, 'Babylon is fallen, is fallen, that great city, because she made all nations drink of the wine of the wrath of her fornication.'

⁹And the third angel followed them, saying with a loud voice, 'If any man worship the beast and his image, and receive his mark in his forehead, or in his hand, ¹⁰the same shall drink of the wine of the wrath of God, which is poured out without mixture into the cup of his indignation; and he shall be tormented with fire and brimstone in the presence

of the holy angels, and in the presence of the Lamb. ¹¹And the smoke of their torment ascendeth up for ever and ever; and they have no rest day nor night, who worship the beast and his image, and whosoever receiveth the mark of his name.'

¹²Here is the patience of the saints: here are they that keep the commandments of God, and the faith of Jesus.

¹³And I heard a voice from heaven saying unto me, 'Write, Blessed are the dead which die in the Lord from henceforth.' 'Yea,' saith the Spirit, 'that they may rest from their labours; and their works do follow them.'

¹⁴And I looked, and behold a white cloud, and upon the cloud one sat like unto the Son of man, having on his head a golden crown, and in his hand a sharp sickle. ¹⁵And another angel came out of the temple, crying with a loud voice to him that sat on the cloud, 'Thrust in thy sickle, and reap; for the time is come for thee to reap; for the harvest of the earth is ripe.' ¹⁶And he that sat on the cloud thrust in his sickle on the earth; and the earth was reaped.

¹⁷And another angel came out of the temple which is in heaven, he also having a sharp sickle. ¹⁸And another angel came out from the altar, which had power over fire; and cried with a loud cry to him that had the sharp sickle, saying, 'Thrust in thy sharp sickle, and gather the clusters of the vine of the earth; for her grapes are fully ripe.' ¹⁹And the angel thrust in his sickle into the earth, and gathered the vine of the earth, and cast it into the great winepress of the wrath of God. ²⁰And the winepress was trodden without the city, and blood came out of the winepress, even unto the horse bridles, by the space of a thousand and six hundred furlongs.

15 And I saw another sign in heaven, great and marvellous, seven angels having the seven last plagues; for in them is filled up the wrath of God.

²And I saw as it were a sea of glass mingled with fire; and them that had gotten the victory over the beast, and over his image, and over his mark, and over the number of his name, stand on the sea of glass, having the harps of God. ³And they sing the song of Moses the servant of God, and the song of the Lamb, saying,

> Great and marvellous are thy works,
> Lord God Almighty;
> just and true are thy ways,
> thou King of saints.
> ⁴Who shall not fear thee, O Lord,
> and glorify thy name?
> For thou only art holy;
> for all nations shall come and worship before thee;
> for thy judgments are made manifest.

⁵And after that I looked, and, behold, the temple of the tabernacle of the testimony in heaven was opened. ⁶And the seven angels came out of the temple, having the seven plagues, clothed in pure and white linen, and having their breasts girded with golden girdles. ⁷And one of the four beasts gave unto the seven angels seven golden vials full of the wrath of God, who liveth for ever and ever. ⁸And the temple was filled with smoke from the glory of God, and from his power; and no man was able to enter into the temple, till the seven plagues of the seven angels were fulfilled.

16 And I heard a great voice out of the temple saying to the seven angels, 'Go your ways, and pour out the vials of the wrath of God upon the earth.'

²And the first went, and poured out his vial upon the earth; and there fell a noisome and grievous sore upon the men which had the mark of the beast, and upon them which worshipped his image.

³And the second angel poured out his vial upon the sea; and it became as the blood of a dead man; and every living soul died in the sea.

⁴And the third angel poured out his vial upon the rivers and fountains of waters; and they became blood. ⁵And I heard the angel of the waters say, 'Thou art righteous, O Lord, which art, and wast, and shalt be, because thou hast judged thus. ⁶For they have shed the blood of saints and prophets, and thou hast given them blood to drink; for they are worthy.' ⁷And I heard another out of the altar say, 'Even so, Lord God Almighty, true and righteous are thy judgments.'

⁸And the fourth angel poured out his vial upon the sun; and power was given unto him to scorch men with fire. ⁹And men were scorched with great heat, and blasphemed the name of God, which hath power over these plagues; and they repented not to give him glory.

¹⁰And the fifth angel poured out his vial upon the seat of the beast; and his kingdom was full of darkness; and they gnawed their tongues for pain, ¹¹and blasphemed the God of heaven because of their pains and their sores, and repented not of their deeds.

¹²And the sixth angel poured out his vial upon the great

river Euphrates; and the water thereof was dried up, that the way of the kings of the east might be prepared. ¹³And I saw three unclean spirits like frogs come out of the mouth of the dragon, and out of the mouth of the beast, and out of the mouth of the false prophet. ¹⁴For they are the spirits of devils, working miracles, which go forth unto the kings of the earth and of the whole world, to gather them to the battle of that great day of God Almighty. ¹⁵'Behold, I come as a thief. Blessed is he that watcheth, and keepeth his garments, lest he walk naked, and they see his shame.' ¹⁶And he gathered them together into a place called in the Hebrew tongue Armageddon.

¹⁷And the seventh angel poured out his vial into the air; and there came a great voice out of the temple of heaven, from the throne, saying, 'It is done.' ¹⁸And there were voices, and thunders, and lightnings; and there was a great earthquake, such as was not since men were upon the earth, so mighty an earthquake, and so great. ¹⁹And the great city was divided into three parts, and the cities of the nations fell; and great Babylon came in remembrance before God, to give unto her the cup of the wine of the fierceness of his wrath. ²⁰And every island fled away, and the mountains were not found. ²¹And there fell upon men a great hail out of heaven, every stone about the weight of a talent; and men blasphemed God because of the plague of the hail; for the plague thereof was exceeding great.

17 And there came one of the seven angels which had the seven vials, and talked with me, saying unto me, 'Come hither; I will shew unto thee the judgment of the great whore that sitteth upon many waters, ² with whom the kings of the earth have committed fornication, and the inhabitants of the earth have been made drunk with the wine of her fornication.' ³ So he carried me away in the spirit into the wilderness; and I saw a woman sit upon a scarlet coloured beast, full of names of blasphemy, having seven heads and ten horns. ⁴And the woman was arrayed in purple and scarlet colour, and decked with gold and precious stones and pearls, having a golden cup in her hand full of abominations and filthiness of her fornication: ⁵ and upon her forehead was a name written, 'MYSTERY, BABYLON THE GREAT, THE MOTHER OF HARLOTS AND ABOMINATIONS OF THE EARTH.' ⁶And I saw the woman drunken with the blood of the saints, and with the blood of the martyrs of Jesus; and when I saw her, I wondered with great admiration.

⁷And the angel said unto me, 'Wherefore didst thou marvel? I will tell thee the mystery of the woman, and of the beast that carrieth her, which hath the seven heads and ten horns. ⁸ The beast that thou sawest was, and is not; and shall ascend out of the bottomless pit, and go into perdition; and they that dwell on the earth shall wonder, whose names were not written in the book of life from the foundation of the world, when they behold the beast that was, and is not, and yet is.

⁹ 'And here is the mind which hath wisdom. The seven heads are seven mountains, on which the woman sitteth. ¹⁰And there are seven kings: five are fallen, and one is, and

the other is not yet come; and when he cometh, he must continue a short space. ¹¹And the beast that was, and is not, even he is the eighth, and is of the seven, and goeth into perdition. ¹²And the ten horns which thou sawest are ten kings, which have received no kingdom as yet; but receive power as kings one hour with the beast. ¹³These have one mind, and shall give their power and strength unto the beast. ¹⁴These shall make war with the Lamb, and the Lamb shall overcome them; for he is Lord of lords, and King of kings; and they that are with him are called, and chosen, and faithful.'

¹⁵And he saith unto me, 'The waters which thou sawest, where the whore sitteth, are peoples, and multitudes, and nations, and tongues. ¹⁶And the ten horns which thou sawest upon the beast, these shall hate the whore, and shall make her desolate and naked, and shall eat her flesh, and burn her with fire. ¹⁷For God hath put in their hearts to fulfil his will, and to agree, and give their kingdom unto the beast, until the words of God shall be fulfilled. ¹⁸And the woman which thou sawest is that great city, which reigneth over the kings of the earth.'

18

And after these things I saw another angel come down from heaven, having great power; and the earth was lightened with his glory. ²And he cried mightily with a strong voice, saying, 'Babylon the great is fallen, is fallen, and is become the habitation of devils, and the hold of every foul spirit, and a cage of every unclean and hateful bird. ³For all nations have drunk of the wine of the wrath of her fornication, and the kings of the earth have committed fornication with her, and the merchants of the earth are waxed rich through the abundance of her delicacies.'

⁴And I heard another voice from heaven, saying, 'Come out of her, my people, that ye be not partakers of her sins, and that ye receive not of her plagues. ⁵For her sins have reached unto heaven, and God hath remembered her iniquities. ⁶Reward her even as she rewarded you, and double unto her double according to her works; in the cup which she hath filled fill to her double. ⁷How much she hath glorified herself, and lived deliciously, so much torment and sorrow give her; for she saith in her heart, I sit a queen, and am no widow, and shall see no sorrow. ⁸Therefore shall her plagues come in one day, death, and mourning, and famine; and she shall be utterly burned with fire; for strong is the Lord God who judgeth her.'

⁹And the kings of the earth, who have committed fornication and lived deliciously with her, shall bewail her, and lament for her, when they shall see the smoke of her burning, ¹⁰standing afar off for the fear of her torment, saying, 'Alas, alas, that great city Babylon, that mighty city! For in one hour is thy judgment come.'

¹¹And the merchants of the earth shall weep and mourn over her; for no man buyeth their merchandise any more: ¹²the merchandise of gold, and silver, and precious stones, and of pearls, and fine linen, and purple, and silk, and scarlet, and all thyine wood, and all manner vessels of ivory, and all manner vessels of most precious wood, and of brass, and iron, and marble, ¹³and cinnamon, and odours, and ointments, and frankincense, and wine, and oil, and fine flour, and wheat, and beasts, and sheep, and horses, and chariots, and slaves, and souls of men.

¹⁴'And the fruits that thy soul lusted after are departed from thee, and all things which were dainty and goodly are departed from thee, and thou shalt find them no more at all.'

¹⁵The merchants of these things, which were made rich by her, shall stand afar off for the fear of her torment, weeping and wailing, ¹⁶and saying, 'Alas, alas, that great city, that was clothed in fine linen, and purple, and scarlet, and decked with gold, and precious stones, and pearls! ¹⁷For in one hour so great riches is come to nought.' And every shipmaster, and all the company in ships, and sailors, and as many as trade by sea, stood afar off, ¹⁸and cried when they saw the smoke of her burning, saying, 'What city is like unto this great city!' ¹⁹And they cast dust on their heads, and cried, weeping and wailing, saying, 'Alas, alas, that great city, wherein were made rich all that had ships in the sea by reason of her costliness! For in one hour is she made desolate.'

²⁰Rejoice over her, thou heaven, and ye holy apostles and prophets; for God hath avenged you on her. ²¹And a mighty angel took up a stone like a great millstone, and cast it into

the sea, saying, 'Thus with violence shall that great city Babylon be thrown down, and shall be found no more at all. ²²And the voice of harpers, and musicians, and of pipers, and trumpeters, shall be heard no more at all in thee; and no craftsman, of whatsoever craft he be, shall be found any more in thee; and the sound of a millstone shall be heard no more at all in thee; ²³ and the light of a candle shall shine no more at all in thee; and the voice of the bridegroom and of the bride shall be heard no more at all in thee; for thy merchants were the great men of the earth; for by thy sorceries were all nations deceived. ²⁴And in her was found the blood of prophets, and of saints, and of all that were slain upon the earth.'

19 And after these things I heard a great voice of much people in heaven, saying, 'Alleluia; Salvation, and glory, and honour, and power, unto the Lord our God; ²for true and righteous are his judgments; for he hath judged the great whore, which did corrupt the earth with her fornication, and hath avenged the blood of his servants at her hand.'

³And again they said, 'Alleluia.' And her smoke rose up for ever and ever. ⁴And the four and twenty elders and the four beasts fell down and worshipped God that sat on the throne, saying, 'Amen; Alleluia.'

⁵And a voice came out of the throne, saying, 'Praise our God, all ye his servants, and ye that fear him, both small and great.' ⁶And I heard as it were the voice of a great multitude, and as the voice of many waters, and as the voice of mighty thunderings, saying, 'Alleluia: for the Lord God omnipotent reigneth. ⁷Let us be glad and rejoice, and give honour to him; for the marriage of the Lamb is come, and his wife hath made herself ready. ⁸And to her was granted that she should be arrayed in fine linen, clean and white; for the fine linen is the righteousness of saints.'

⁹And he saith unto me, 'Write, Blessed are they which are called unto the marriage supper of the Lamb.' And he saith unto me, 'These are the true sayings of God.' ¹⁰And I fell at his feet to worship him. And he said unto me, 'See thou do it not: I am thy fellowservant, and of thy brethren that have the testimony of Jesus; worship God, for the testimony of Jesus is the spirit of prophecy.'

¹¹And I saw heaven opened, and behold a white horse; and he that sat upon him was called Faithful and True, and

in righteousness he doth judge and make war. [12]His eyes were as a flame of fire, and on his head were many crowns; and he had a name written, that no man knew, but he himself. [13]And he was clothed with a vesture dipped in blood; and his name is called The Word of God. [14]And the armies which were in heaven followed him upon white horses, clothed in fine linen, white and clean. [15]And out of his mouth goeth a sharp sword, that with it he should smite the nations; and he shall rule them with a rod of iron; and he treadeth the winepress of the fierceness and wrath of Almighty God. [16]And he hath on his vesture and on his thigh a name written, 'KING OF KINGS, AND LORD OF LORDS.'

[17]And I saw an angel standing in the sun; and he cried with a loud voice, saying to all the fowls that fly in the midst of heaven, 'Come and gather yourselves together unto the supper of the great God; [18]that ye may eat the flesh of kings, and the flesh of captains, and the flesh of mighty men, and the flesh of horses, and of them that sit on them, and the flesh of all men, both free and bond, both small and great.' [19]And I saw the beast, and the kings of the earth, and their armies, gathered together to make war against him that sat on the horse, and against his army. [20]And the beast was taken, and with him the false prophet that wrought miracles before him, with which he deceived them that had received the mark of the beast, and them that worshipped his image. These both were cast alive into a lake of fire burning with brimstone. [21]And the remnant were slain with the sword of him that sat upon the horse, which sword proceeded out of his mouth; and all the fowls were filled with their flesh.

20 And I saw an angel come down from heaven, having the key of the bottomless pit and a great chain in his hand. ²And he laid hold on the dragon, that old serpent, which is the Devil, and Satan, and bound him a thousand years, ³and cast him into the bottomless pit, and shut him up, and set a seal upon him, that he should deceive the nations no more, till the thousand years should be fulfilled; and after that he must be loosed a little season.

⁴And I saw thrones, and they sat upon them, and judgment was given unto them; and I saw the souls of them that were beheaded for the witness of Jesus, and for the word of God, and which had not worshipped the beast, neither his image, neither had received his mark upon their foreheads, or in their hands; and they lived and reigned with Christ a thousand years. ⁵But the rest of the dead lived not again until the thousand years were finished. This is the first resurrection. ⁶Blessed and holy is he that hath part in the first resurrection; on such the second death hath no power, but they shall be priests of God and of Christ, and shall reign with him a thousand years.

⁷And when the thousand years are expired, Satan shall be loosed out of his prison, ⁸and shall go out to deceive the nations which are in the four quarters of the earth, Gog and Magog, to gather them together to battle; the number of whom is as the sand of the sea. ⁹And they went up on the breadth of the earth, and compassed the camp of the saints about, and the beloved city; and fire came down from God out of heaven, and devoured them. ¹⁰And the devil that deceived them was cast into the lake of fire and brimstone,

where the beast and the false prophet are, and shall be tormented day and night for ever and ever.

¹¹And I saw a great white throne, and him that sat on it, from whose face the earth and the heaven fled away; and there was found no place for them. ¹²And I saw the dead, small and great, stand before God; and the books were opened; and another book was opened, which is the book of life; and the dead were judged out of those things which were written in the books, according to their works. ¹³And the sea gave up the dead which were in it; and death and hell delivered up the dead which were in them; and they were judged every man according to their works. ¹⁴And death and hell were cast into the lake of fire. This is the second death. ¹⁵And whosoever was not found written in the book of life was cast into the lake of fire.

21 And I saw a new heaven and a new earth; for the first heaven and the first earth were passed away; and there was no more sea. ²And I John saw the holy city, new Jerusalem, coming down from God out of heaven, prepared as a bride adorned for her husband. ³And I heard a great voice out of heaven saying, 'Behold, the tabernacle of God is with men, and he will dwell with them, and they shall be his people, and God himself shall be with them, and be their God. ⁴And God shall wipe away all tears from their eyes; and there shall be no more death, neither sorrow, nor crying, neither shall there be any more pain; for the former things are passed away.'

⁵And he that sat upon the throne said, 'Behold, I make all things new.' And he said unto me, 'Write: for these words are true and faithful.' ⁶And he said unto me, 'It is done. I am Alpha and Omega, the beginning and the end. I will give unto him that is athirst of the fountain of the water of life freely. ⁷He that overcometh shall inherit all things; and I will be his God, and he shall be my son. ⁸But the fearful, and unbelieving, and the abominable, and murderers, and whoremongers, and sorcerers, and idolaters, and all liars, shall have their part in the lake which burneth with fire and brimstone; which is the second death.'

⁹And there came unto me one of the seven angels which had the seven vials full of the seven last plagues, and talked with me, saying, 'Come hither, I will shew thee the bride, the Lamb's wife.' ¹⁰And he carried me away in the spirit to a great and high mountain, and shewed me that great city, the holy Jerusalem, descending out of heaven from God, ¹¹having the

glory of God; and her light was like unto a stone most precious, even like a jasper stone, clear as crystal; ¹²and had a wall great and high, and had twelve gates, and at the gates twelve angels, and names written thereon, which are the names of the twelve tribes of the children of Israel: ¹³on the east three gates; on the north three gates; on the south three gates; and on the west three gates. ¹⁴And the wall of the city had twelve foundations, and in them the names of the twelve apostles of the Lamb.

¹⁵And he that talked with me had a golden reed to measure the city, and the gates thereof, and the wall thereof. ¹⁶And the city lieth foursquare, and the length is as large as the breadth; and he measured the city with the reed, twelve thousand furlongs. The length and the breadth and the height of it are equal. ¹⁷And he measured the wall thereof, an hundred and forty and four cubits, according to the measure of a man, that is, of the angel. ¹⁸And the building of the wall of it was of jasper; and the city was pure gold, like unto clear glass. ¹⁹And the foundations of the wall of the city were garnished with all manner of precious stones. The first foundation was jasper; the second, sapphire; the third, a chalcedony; the fourth, an emerald; ²⁰the fifth, sardonyx; the sixth, sardius; the seventh, chrysolite; the eighth, beryl; the ninth, a topaz; the tenth, a chrysoprasus; the eleventh, a jacinth; the twelfth, an amethyst. ²¹And the twelve gates were twelve pearls; every several gate was of one pearl; and the street of the city was pure gold, as it were transparent glass.

²²And I saw no temple therein; for the Lord God Almighty and the Lamb are the temple of it. ²³And the city had no need

of the sun, neither of the moon, to shine in it: for the glory of God did lighten it, and the Lamb is the light thereof. ²⁴And the nations of them which are saved shall walk in the light of it; and the kings of the earth do bring their glory and honour into it. ²⁵And the gates of it shall not be shut at all by day; for there shall be no night there. ²⁶And they shall bring the glory and honour of the nations into it. ²⁷And there shall in no wise enter into it any thing that defileth, neither whatsoever worketh abomination, or maketh a lie; but they which are written in the Lamb's book of life.

22 And he shewed me a pure river of water of life, clear as crystal, proceeding out of the throne of God and of the Lamb. ²In the midst of the street of it, and on either side of the river, was there the tree of life, which bare twelve manner of fruits, and yielded her fruit every month; and the leaves of the tree were for the healing of the nations. ³And there shall be no more curse, but the throne of God and of the Lamb shall be in it; and his servants shall serve him; ⁴and they shall see his face; and his name shall be in their foreheads. ⁵And there shall be no night there; and they need no candle, neither light of the sun; for the Lord God giveth them light; and they shall reign for ever and ever.

⁶And he said unto me, 'These sayings are faithful and true; and the Lord God of the holy prophets sent his angel to shew unto his servants the things which must shortly be done. ⁷Behold, I come quickly; blessed is he that keepeth the sayings of the prophecy of this book.'

⁸And I John saw these things, and heard them. And when I had heard and seen, I fell down to worship before the feet of the angel which shewed me these things. ⁹Then saith he unto me, 'See thou do it not; for I am thy fellowservant, and of thy brethren the prophets, and of them which keep the sayings of this book: worship God.' ¹⁰And he saith unto me, 'Seal not the sayings of the prophecy of this book; for the time is at hand. ¹¹He that is unjust, let him be unjust still; and he which is filthy, let him be filthy still; and he that is righteous, let him be righteous still; and he that is holy, let him be holy still.

¹²'And, behold, I come quickly; and my reward is with

me, to give every man according as his work shall be. ¹³ I am Alpha and Omega, the beginning and the end, the first and the last.'

¹⁴ Blessed are they that do his commandments, that they may have right to the tree of life, and may enter in through the gates into the city. ¹⁵ For without are dogs, and sorcerers, and whoremongers, and murderers, and idolaters, and whosoever loveth and maketh a lie.

¹⁶ 'I Jesus have sent mine angel to testify unto you these things in the churches. I am the root and the offspring of David, and the bright and morning star.' ¹⁷ And the Spirit and the bride say, 'Come.' And let him that heareth say, 'Come.' And let him that is athirst come. And whosoever will, let him take the water of life freely. ¹⁸ For I testify unto every man that heareth the words of the prophecy of this book, if any man shall add unto these things, God shall add unto him the plagues that are written in this book. ¹⁹ And if any man shall take away from the words of the book of this prophecy, God shall take away his part out of the book of life, and out of the holy city, and from the things which are written in this book. ²⁰ He which testifieth these things saith, 'Surely I come quickly.' Amen. Even so, come, Lord Jesus. ²¹ The grace of our Lord Jesus Christ be with you all. Amen.